T0298985

# Implementing the Public Finance Management Act in South Africa:

## How Far Are We?

## by Russell Wildeman and Wellington Jogo

Economic Governance Programme, Idasa

2012

Published by Idasa, 357 Visagie Street, Pretoria 0001

© Idasa 2012

ISBN 978-1-920409-75-3

First published 2012

Editing by Hilda Hermann

Design, layout and production by Bronwen Müller

Cover by Bronwen Müller

All rights reserved. No part of this publication may be reproduced or transmitted, in any form or by any means, without prior permission from the publishers.

# Contents

Page

# Tables                                                    Page

# Figures                                                   Page

# Acknowledgements

This report is part of a project that was funded by the Ford Foundation, Southern Africa. The project examined the democratisation of economic governance in South Africa post-apartheid. This project had three components, namely, the development of an economic policy literacy course for civil society organisations an examination of budget reform in the post-1994 period, and an examination of the implementation of the Public Finance Management Act (No. 1 of 1999).

We are grateful for the consistent financial support of the Ford Foundation, which enabled us to complete this and the other two outputs. We are certain that this paper contributes to better understanding the evolution of the public finance regime in South Africa in the post-1994 period. Through further funding support from the Foundation, we are developing an economic policy literacy course for local government policy and civil society actors, and the insights we have developed through this research are being used in the development of course materials.

We are grateful for the independent comments provided by Ms Tania Ajam, Mr Mario Claasen and Mr Ralph Mathekga. These have enabled us to fine-tune the paper and incorporate most of their feedback. We are also grateful for the comments and feedback provided by Dr Johann Stegmann of the Western Cape Provincial Treasury. What we found most useful from the comments was the suggestion that we extend the period under consideration to cover implementation up until 2010. This has added further quality and perspective to the paper.

Finally, we wish to extend our thanks to our colleagues in the Economic Governance Programme of Idasa who read various versions of the document. This made the completion of the short paper a challenging but enjoyable task.

Russell Wildeman and Wellington Jogo
January 2012

# Authors

Russell Wildeman is the Programme Manager for Idasa's Economic Governance Programme.

Wellington Jogo is the former Project Head of the Economic Governance Programme's Public Finance project and now works as an Associate Economist at Bioversity International, Uganda.

# Executive summary

The research reported in this paper is part of a Ford Foundation-funded project, which examines how the democratisation process in South Africa, after 1994, impacted on economic governance more broadly and financial governance more specifically. In this report, we review the implementation of the Public Finance Management Act (PFMA), 1999 (No. 1 of 1999), thus focusing our enquiry on the development and reform of financial governance arrangements after 2000. The period under review is 2000 to 2010, even though the actual interviews for the research were concluded in 2009. We extended the period under review because important policy, legislative and operational changes occurred in 2009 and 2010 that have a direct bearing on the present and future implementation fortunes of the PFMA.

The specific objectives of the research are:

- to better understand the relationship between the actual law, its implementation, and whether ten years of implementation have changed key provisions of the law;

- to review the implementation evidence on the three budget outcomes – aggregate fiscal discipline, allocative efficiency and operational efficiency – and enquire whether established descriptions and explanations of these outcomes still hold, or, whether a more refined description is needed;

- to identify the most important implementation successes and challenges during the period of the review; and

- to develop a set of recommendations detailing what financial governance practices could be emulated, and what practices should be avoided, especially for countries in the region that are planning to undertake similar reforms.

On the first objective, the PFMA has remained substantively unchanged despite the implementation challenges faced over the last ten years. Our overall conclusion is that the law is well written, is flexible enough to anticipate policy changes, and the key ingredients of the law have been unchallenged and unchanged over the ten-year period of review. Recently, there have been calls for the amendment of the law to deal with the poor disciplinary environment in departments, but the implementation evidence that we present does not support this view. Challenges relate mostly to poor quality finance staff, instability in staffing arrangements, variable accounting officer (AO) performance, and poor back-up systems (information technology (IT), monitoring and evaluation (M&E) and non-financial reporting more generally), rather than provisions of the policy that are impossible to implement, or, which were poorly conceived and, hence, impractical to implement. In other words, the people and systems that make full implementation of the PFMA possible have not been realised. There were instances where political office bearers questioned the 'onerous' reporting requirements of the law, implying that some kind of compliance mentality exists, but this did not lead to a reduction in the scope of the information that departmental entities have to provide. What also enabled the framework legislation to remain relatively unscathed is the fact that the accompanying Treasury Regulations and circulars from the National Treasury tackled the practical aspects of the law head on. Our overall conclusion is that the implementation of the PFMA has had little impact on the integrity of the law itself. This view may yet change, but we are clearly not facing a situation where implementation results have forced a rethink of the overall design of the PFMA.

The second objective looked at the implementation of the PFMA from the point of the view of the three budget outcomes: aggregate fiscal discipline, allocative efficiency and operational efficiency. We wanted to verify whether the now established narrative, which asserts that we have succeeded in living within our means (fiscal discipline) and moving resources to where they are needed (allocative efficiency), and that our value-for-money spending is poor (operational efficiency), still provides an accurate description of the state of our public finance system.

Our review confirms that aggregate fiscal discipline has been achieved as a result of the introduction of the Medium-Term Expenditure Framework (MTEF) budget system, strong political backing and leadership of reform initiatives, and consensus-building efforts in intergovernmental fora aimed at preserving fiscal prudence across the three levels of government.

On the issue of allocative efficiency, the government has made great strides and our review concurs with most other reviews on this topic. The shifts in spending across functions and in the composition of spending are partly supported by the fact that the same political party has been in power since 1994, thus ensuring some policy stability in the way resources are allocated. In our review, we argue that allocative efficiency gains at the sub-national level (provincial government) did not take place because of existing practices and efforts at the provincial level. In fact, we argue that intergovernmental fora have played a substantial role in effecting resources shifts at the provincial level in much the same way the old Function Committee system redistributed resources across provinces. While this was good practice at the start of the new democracy, where aggressive re-prioritisation was needed, policy and financing realities now require a different approach to how resources are allocated at the sub-national level. Intergovernmental fora may have brought about significant shifts, but their operation, in part, undermined the ability of provinces to tackle their own resources agendas. Furthermore, because of the small discretionary fiscal space at the provincial level, there has been little incentive to develop strategic planning skills. The absence or short supply of these skills at the provincial level has further undermined the ability of provinces to address province-specific issues. Hence, instead of being a vital and vibrant partner in the intergovernmental system, provinces have been reduced to administrations and there is little evidence to the contrary to suggest this is likely to change in the near future.

Operational efficiency gains have been unimpressive and, in this regard, we concur with other reviews. One of the key reasons for this state of affairs is that efficiency measures were unavailable and only introduced in the system in 2008. This meant that departments had no benchmark of their actual performance, other than annual audited financial statements. While the latter are vital from a financial governance point of view, from a performance perspective it is an insufficient measure of how well departments execute their financial management responsibilities. Other factors impacting on the poor performance of departments are variable AO performance, political interference in the in-year management of budgets, and insular departments that do not engage fully and consistently with the Standing Committee on Public Accounts (SCOPA) and Auditor-General (AG) recommendations, and that have no meaningful and enduring contact with citizens.

The third objective of the review examined key implementation successes and challenges, and considered whether new policy and legislative developments could positively influence present and future implementation trends. On the implementation successes, we concluded that the PFMA has fundamentally altered the overall reporting and budget information environment in the public service. Although there are questions about the overall quality of such reports and disputes over whether the reporting burden is disproportionate, it is nearly impossible to resist the proposition that the PFMA generated more budget information (financial and non-financial), which is now freely available to parliamentarians and the broader public. It is not only that more information is available, but also that such information is provided timely as per the implementation schedules laid out in the PFMA. This transpired despite initial fears that the implementation schedules for submission of financial and consolidated reports were too punishing. Secondly, the PFMA and associated regulations have undoubtedly contributed to improved transparency in the budget information that is available and presented in official government documents. External and objective evidence for this is our comparative standing among both developed and developing countries as measured by the Open Budget Index (OBI). In the 2010 version of the OBI, South Africa was ranked the most open and transparent provider of budget information, making this information widely available to the media and the public in general, and producing national budget documentation of outstanding quality.

Arguably, the biggest implementation success is the careful manner in which the National Treasury supported and built the capacity of officials in treasuries and service delivery departments. It adopted a model based on the careful design of information templates and detailed circulars, thus minimising the level of subjectivity in the reporting of important financial and non-financial data. We think this was an entirely appropriate response at the start of the financial governance reforms and is partly the reason why the government was able to meet most of the information commitments spelled out in the Constitution and the PFMA. This is a remarkable success story of thoughtful and patient capacity building, and one that should be emulated elsewhere. We do, however, raise questions about whether such a capacity model can move officials to start managing for results. Our conclusion is that this fuller implementation and interpretation of the PFMA requires capable administrative leaders, and that a template-led capacity-building strategy may not work.

On implementation challenges, it became clear that a key challenge relates to the inability of departments to establish a coherent and comprehensive M&E system. The AG and external commentators routinely refer to the poor quality of the indicators, their arbitrariness, and the fact that these indicators do not meaningfully measure the service in question. This brings us to our second implementation challenge, namely the frequency and rate at which departments actively respond to recommendations made to them by the AG. There appears to be a broken chain between the recommendations of the AG, the actions and discussions in the various public accounts committees in Parliament and provincial legislatures, and the remedial actions that should happen in affected departments. The third implementation challenge we want to highlight is the reality where citizens and civil society as a whole are not involved in allocation decisions or consulted on operational matters. The overall picture that emerges is one of insular departments that are closed off from reality, thus making the task of redesigning service delivery mechanisms that much harder, if not impossible.

In response to the implementation challenges, our review considered the potential impact of new laws, policies and recent results from the reports of the AG on the implementation of the PFMA. We concluded that the introduction of unit cost methodologies could potentially wring massive savings from the system. Parliament's new role in the budget process should intensify its scrutiny of existing PFMA-legislated documents, and the trend towards performance auditing is deeply encouraging and must be extended to as many departments as possible.

Finally, on practices to emulate, we recommend that other countries in the region consider a model of capacity building similar to the one led by the National Treasury. In essence, this is a template-driven approach that eliminates departmental-specific weaknesses in the provision of information required by law. We also recommend that countries keep to their financial reform targets; if possible, introduce an efficiency tool like the financial maturity capability tool to incrementally measure departments' performance; and the use of intergovernmental and inter-sectoral fora to discuss policy and financing issues.

On practices to avoid, we caution against financial and budget reforms that happens at too rapid a pace, and which make the deepening of such reforms difficult; weak co-ordination among oversight, constitutional bodies and central government that dilute the force of the work done by some agencies must be avoided at all cost; adopting a system where sub-national government has extensive expenditure responsibilities, but no revenue-raising powers, thus leading to the formations of lacklustre administrations shorn of any incentive to address local issues; and finally, because of the rapid pace of reforms, the setting in of a compliance mentality that consists of separating financial governance and service delivery mandates and obligations.

South Africa has a long way to go to ensuring that financial reforms are translated into service delivery gains. Progress in implementing reforms and making sure that citizens benefit is proving harder, yet the convergence of various government agencies in addressing financial governance is beginning to inspire the kind of confidence needed to overcome financial governance challenges. Despite the challenges, on balance, it appears that the PFMA has begun to make a difference and, if properly implemented, may still provide the ground for a fundamental transformation of public sector service delivery.

# Introduction

Some public policy theorists (Brynard, 2005) argue that the implementation of policies offers a rich template for reflecting on policies, and that implementation should not be seen as the end of the policy-making stage. This view disputes the idea that the policy-making process is complete once a piece of legislation is signed into law. Implementation, according to these theorists, is not the opposite of the idea-forming dimension of policy making, but is itself capable of generating noteworthy policy ideas and changes. It is for this reason that the implementation of policies is such an important research area and none more so than the framework public finance legislation introduced in South Africa in 2000.

The PFMA was first implemented in April 2000 and, until the end of 2010, was subjected to a series of amendments reflecting important policy and legislative changes.[i] The PFMA repealed the then Exchequer Act (No. 66 of 1975) that previously governed public financial management in South Africa. Under the exchequer regime, public financial management emphasised expenditure control rather than managing funds for service delivery improvement. The focus on inputs (how much money a department intends to spend) made it difficult to measure the efficiency and effectiveness of public spending. The lack of non-financial information on service delivery outputs hampered the ability of public-service managers, executives and legislators to make informed decisions on the effective and efficient use of public money (Nkoana & Bokoda, 2009).

By its very nature, the PFMA is regarded as framework legislation, which means the actual details of implementation are worked out in a series of regulations and directives produced by the National Treasury. Hence, the PFMA and its implementation processes perfectly complement the philosophical view that implementation is not the opposite of policy making, and, by itself, contributes substantially to formal policy making.

While the PFMA is a theoretically comprehensive and coherent piece of legislation, any piece of legislation is only as good as its implementation. Although several studies have argued that the Act improved account-ability and budget implementation (Folscher & Cole, 2006), to date, few independent studies have been done to critically document the implemen-tation challenges and successes of the new public finance management regime in South Africa in treasury departments and service delivery depart-ments. Against this background, the aim of the present review is two-fold: one, to describe the consensus thinking that has developed around the implementation of the PFMA, and using our interview data and external sources of information to establish whether this consensus view still holds, or whether changes and refinement of these views are called for. Two, we review what we consider the most important implementation successes and challenges of the PFMA and enquire whether recent legislative and policy developments could potentially influence the way we view imple-mentation challenges. The latter is viewed against a background of con-sistent capacity development led by the National Treasury in national and provincial governments, and we explore the benefits and limits of such a structured capacity-building process.

What is the consensus view on the implementation of the PFMA? This consensus view is represented well in an article by Folscher and Cole (2006), where the authors note that aggregate fiscal discipline and alloca-tive efficiency have largely been achieved under the new public finance regime, while operational efficiency, or the value-for-money principle, has not worked out as well as policy makers intended.[ii] Reasons for the present state of affairs range from the absence of the right people for the job at hand; not having the right systems to match the legislative and philo-sophical sophistication of the Act; to maturing budget institutions, rules and roles that need time before their true impact can be felt.

How coherent and tight is this narrative and are there implementation details that alter this view of the implementation of the PFMA? Or is it the case that this view prevails, but there are important nuances that were pre-viously not accounted for? Are the PFMA and its heavy information and accountability demands part of the reasons for the poor state of service delivery in key portfolios in South Africa? How high a standard does the PFMA set and should we temper our expectations about the government's ability to improve services in the next five to ten years? In other words, are commentators' expectations of what the public finance system can deliver realistic?

# Methods of data collection

To answer these questions, the Idasa team opted for a structured interview methodology. This was preceded by an extensive literature search that examined studies that deal with the implementation of the PFMA in South Africa and the implementation of finance frameworks in developing countries. We knew we had to interview the lead agency in the formulation and implementation of the PFMA, namely the National Treasury, but we did not know what the balance should be between treasuries and other service delivery departments. In the end, we decided to interview all ten treasuries and focus on three service delivery departments at the national and provincial level. It is obvious to us that any follow-up study must prioritise service delivery departments and how they deal with the twin challenge of implementing the PFMA and executing their service delivery obligations. Nine of the ten treasury responses were obtained using structured telephonic and in-person recorded interviews, while the National Treasury provided detailed written responses to our list of questions. Further follow-up questions were sent to the National Treasury.

The three service delivery departments we chose were the national Department of Education, Gauteng Department of Housing and Local Government and the Mpumalanga Department of Health. While these three departments deliver important policy and service delivery functions, we may have equally chosen three other departments, hence the selection was arbitrarily done. All we wanted to do was to examine how the implementation of the PFMA worked out in departments whose main purpose is policy formulation (national education) and service delivery (provincial housing and health). The national Department of Education opted to provide detailed written responses to our questions, while the two provincial departments participated in recorded telephonic interviews with the Idasa team.

The essence of the treasury questions was to better understand the correlation between the conditions prior to the formulation and implementation of the Act, and what the Act prioritised at the inception phase. Part of the research was also about establishing the uniqueness of the legislation and whether there were key external criteria by which we could judge the success of the implementation of the PFMA. We were also interested in understanding how provincial treasuries were supported, and what the key implementation challenges and successes were during the period 2000 to 2008. In the case of service delivery departments, we wanted to better understand how the reporting burden of the PFMA affects service delivery; key implementation successes and challenges; and which provisions of the PFMA presented them with the greatest implementation challenges.

Following the review of the first draft, reviewers sent extensive suggestions for further reading that were immediately relevant to the topic at hand. One of the suggestions was to extend the coverage of the paper from 2008 to 2010, in order to consider the outcome-driven delivery agreement process and auditing trends in 2009/10 and 2010/11, and how this could potentially affect implementation of the PFMA. In addition, we looked at the Money Bills Amendment Procedure and Related Matters Act, No. 9 of 2009, and how effective implementation of this law could alter future implementation realities for service delivery departments.

# Roadmap of the report

Section 2 of this report reviews existing implementation evidence on the three dimensions of budget outcomes: aggregate fiscal discipline, allocative efficiency and operational efficiency. We rely on interview materials (primary data), existing academic reviews of the PFMA (secondary data) and service delivery data from the Public Service Commission (PSC) to critically examine implementation data. This section also utilises data from the AG reports in 2009 and 2010 for national departments, provincial government and, especially, the provincial departments of education and health. While perhaps not ideal, we deliberately mix the evidence from treasuries and service delivery departments, even though the nature of the challenges faced by these two entities is different. However, when such differences become necessary for the discussion, we indicate clearly that results apply to a treasury or to a service delivery department. This section is aimed at finding a refined description of the status quo regarding the implementation of the Act and tries to answer the question of whether important revisions to the consensus view are needed.

Section 3 examines the key implementation successes and challenges of the PFMA and considers the potential impact of recent policies, laws and auditing trends on the future implementation of the PFMA in service delivery departments. The latter analysis will necessarily be speculative, but supports the view that recent legislative and policy changes are intended to support the fuller implementation of the PFMA. Because of the regional nature of Idasa's work, Section 4 sets out a small number of practices that countries in the region could emulate, as well as practices that should be avoided. These recommendations are intended for developing countries in the region that have embarked on a similar course of financial and budget reforms. Section 5 offers concluding remarks and provides a summary of the main evidence presented in the paper.

# Implementation of the PFMA and the three budget outcomes

Public finance management reform is more than simply altering negative outcomes on the budget. Government spending should benefit citizens, make citizens more prosperous and healthy, and create sustainable sources of revenue that make service delivery predictable. Nonetheless, in the context of our paper, it would be helpful to think about the implementation of the PFMA in terms of the three key budget outcomes: aggregate fiscal discipline, allocative efficiency and operational efficiency. The relative detail accorded to each one depends on progress achieved with each outcome, the level of agreement among respondents about implementation progress thus far, and the availability of external evidence and indicators about progress made in each of the three outcomes.

## Aggregate fiscal discipline

Ajam and Aron (2007) argue that an improvement in the quality of services that the government needs to deliver is crucial to maintain the impressive fiscal stability gains at the macro level. In the same vein, Folscher and Cole (2006:31) maintain that, while fiscal discipline has been achieved and allocative efficiency improved, efficiency concerns at the operational level remain. In an extensive assessment of the South African public finance reforms, the European Commission's 'Republic of South Africa Public Expenditure and Financial Accountability' report concludes that strict fiscal discipline has been maintained through the MTEF framework 'that is effectively applied as an instrument of top-down discipline to the budgetary process'. (European Commission, 2008:14)

The reasons advanced for the success of the government in achieving fiscal discipline range from the development of three-year rolling budgets, the synchronisation of fiscal and monetary policy, and the establishment of intergovernmental fora where political and administrative consensus was sought on key financing issues. A number of indicators can be used to signal the government's fiscal position: the actual balance, the primary balance (non-interest expenditure) or the structural balance (corrected for cyclical movements). Figure 1 provides information on the balance of the consolidated government budget as a percentage of the Gross Domestic Product (GDP) for the period 2000/01 to 2010/11.

**Figure 1: Consolidated government budget balance as a percentage of GDP**

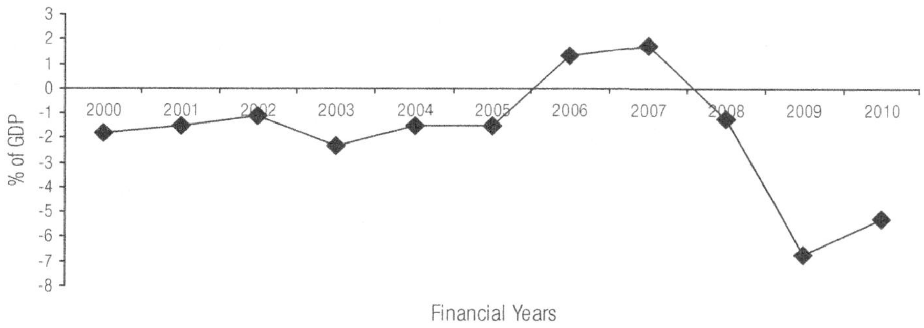

Financial Years

*Sources: National Treasury MTBPS: 2006, 2007, 2009 & 2010*

The trend during the ten-year period is clear: apart from the strong deficits caused by the economic crisis in 2008 and 2009, the government maintained small deficits for the largest part of the period under review. In fact, over the present MTEF, there is a strong tendency to moderate the growth in expenditure and, hence, revert to the default position of the government, which means small absolute deficits on the main budget. In the National Treasury's 2010 Medium Term Budget Policy Statement (MTBPS), the government projects that the budget balance will decline from a figure of 5.3% of GDP in 2010/11 to 3.2% of GDP in 2013/14. However, two critical assumptions are that revenue will have recovered at the end of the previous MTEF and that government will have succeeded in moderating claims on expenditure. Although both assumptions are shaky in the present economic climate, it does not gainsay the results of the financial reform process that consistently brought absolutely low deficits on the consolidated government budget. These numbers confirm the government's commitment to fiscal prudence and affirm what most commentators regard as the country's best success indicator of the financial reform process that began in 1997.

Since the only debate among practitioners is about the kind of fiscal stance the government adopted or should have adopted (conservative versus expansionary), and not about the actual outcome of the reform process, the available evidence is unambiguous and requires little further clarification.

# Allocative efficiency

Allocative efficiency can be conceptualised as having two dimensions: an empirical component (evidence of actual shifts in spending) and a philosophical component (are allocations in line with government policy?). Whereas the indicators for the success of fiscal discipline are straightforward, it would appear that an assessment of progress in achieving allocative efficiency can at best be transient. Dynamic governance and changing policy and political circumstances may dictate different policy priorities. However, because South Africa has been governed by the same political party for the last 16 years, one could make the case that political stability is synonymous with policy stability and, hence, an examination of allocative efficiency gains should be possible.

To make the case for a shift in spending, we examine shifts in spending across functions and across type of spending. The first has direct bearing on so-called priority shifts and should show a clear move towards social services expenditures and away from police and defence types of spending. The second type of spending shift (compositional changes) reflects the government's thinking on the balance among various types of expenditures and what expenditures are valued more in achieving overall policy goals. Table 1 provides information on shifts in spending on functions (expressed as a percentage of GDP) for three periods: 1990/91, 1994/95 and 1997/98.

The three periods signify distinct stages in the development of South Africa's political and public finance systems: 1990 represents the start of the political transition process; 1994, although the year of the first democratic election, almost certainly registers the efforts of the transitional government; and 1997 represents the efforts and changes that took place within the context of the then Function Committee system. Between 1990 and 1994, expected functional shifts materialised, namely better resources for education and social services more generally, and reduced spending on defence. At the end of the 1997/98 financial year, defence spending was trimmed even further, while education spending, although less than its 1994 share, claimed the largest share of government resources. Overall, social services appears to have grown little between 1994 and 1997, partially reflecting the significant freeze on social spending from 1996 onwards.

| Table 1: Functional classification of consolidated national and provincial government expenditure (% of GDP) | | | |
|---|---|---|---|
| Function | 1990/91 | 1994/95 | 1997/98 |
| General public services | 2.4 | 3.0 | 2.1 |
| Defence | 4.0 | 2.9 | 1.7 |
| Public order and safety | 2.4 | 3.2 | 3.0 |
| Education | 6.1 | 7.1 | 6.5 |
| Social security and welfare | 2.0 | 3.1 | 3.0 |
| Other social services | 4.0 | 4.5 | 4.9 |
| Economic services | 4.0 | 4.0 | 3.0 |
| Source: National Treasury MTBPS: 1997 | | | |

Figure 2 represents spending data for the period 1998/99 to 2010/11. It could be read as attempts at allocative efficiency under the new MTEF regime, which first came into being in 1997/98.

Figure 2: Functional classification of consolidated national and provincial government expenditure, 1998/99 to 2010/11 (% of GDP)

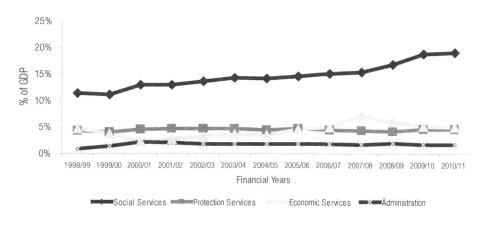

Source: MTBPS, 1999 to 2010
Note: Actual expenditure and final GDP figures used throughout, except for 2010/11

Overall, the share of social services as a percentage of the GDP grew from around 12% in 1998 to close to 20% at the end of 2010/11. This represents consistent growth over the period and provides a direct demonstration of the importance of social services in the government's overall spending plans. For example, at the end of 2010/11, spending on social services was approximately four times the corresponding spending on economic services. All other services were kept constant as a share of the GDP over the corresponding period. Spending shifts during this period took place under the new constitutional arrangement of three interdependent spheres of government. It is important to recognise that South Africa did not devise sectoral spending strategies that were approved at Cabinet level. Shifts in spending were driven by new budget institutions such as the extended Cabinet, joint sectoral fora of national and provincial ministers (MINMECs) and joint cross-sectoral fora of national and provincial political office bearers (10*10, etc.).

While functional shits are clear indicators of allocative efficiency, it is also important to examine shifts in the type of spending across functions. This provides perspective on spending types that the government considers important in realising policy and political goals.

Figure 3 provides spending data for four distinct periods between 1998 and 2009.

**Figure 3: Compositional shifts in spending by type of expenditure for 1998/99, 2003/04, 2006/07 and 2009/10 (% of non-interest expenditure)**

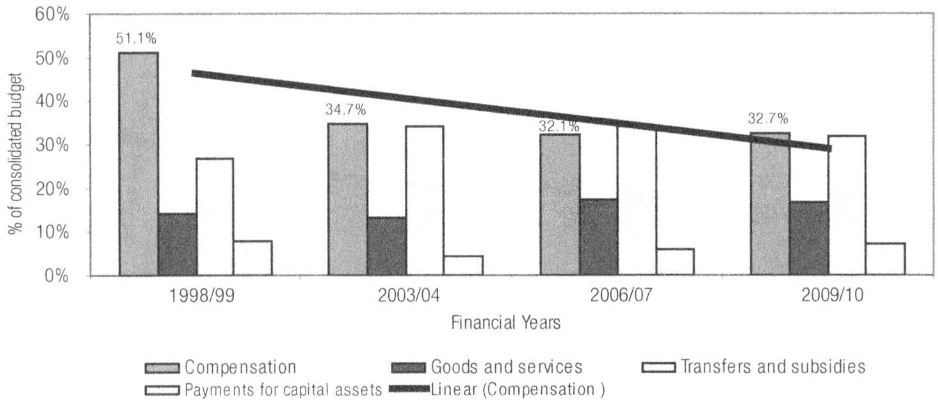

Sources: National Treasury MTPBS: 1999, 2003, 2007 and 2010

The data indicate that expenditure on personnel (salary and other benefits) dropped from 51% in 1998 to 33% in 2009, which represents a massive decline of 18% over this period. In numerous publications and policy pronouncements, the government considered spending on personnel as crowding out investments in infrastructure and other productive economic activities. However, looking at Figure 3, spending on transfers and subsidies – of which the bulk would be social security payments – grew impressively over this period. Expenditure on capital and infrastructure did not prove to be the consistent beneficiary of lower spending on personnel, partly due to the project-driven nature of infrastructure spending and the poor capacity of government departments to spend their allocated capital budgets.

The purpose of this paper is not to establish the net effect of such compositional shifts, but to test whether such shifts confirm the consensus view that we have largely achieved allocative efficiency. We can confirm that substantial functional and compositional shifts in spending took place over the last 15 years. However, the problem with existing mainstream accounts of the implementation of the PFMA is that they do not explain how we arrived at this position,[iii] and whether this situation is stable or bound to change. To answer some of these questions, we reflect on the responses provided by treasuries and service delivery departments. Where possible, we provide external data to back up some claims.

From a careful analysis of the interview data, three key dimensions emerge, which we theorise have an impact on allocative efficiency at the provincial level: a human resources/capacity dimension, a budgetary dimension and a political dimension.

## Human resources/capacity and allocative efficiency

Both national and provincial treasury respondents reflected on the lack of strategic planning skills at the provincial level, and how such deficits hamper the re-prioritisation of budgets. In fact, it is common knowledge that certain provisions of the PFMA were delayed until such time that the government built the necessary skills.

Throughout the interviews with treasuries and service delivery departments, the issue of skills deficits around public finance management was prominent. While turnover of finance staff was important, respondents focused on how existing staff at the provincial level are inept at linking strategic plans to budgets. Box 1 provides a sample of some of their comments.

> **Box 1**
>
> There are usually major shifts between February and November, and that's all over the country, which means that the planning that went into the budget, even for the current year, is not as good as it should be. But it has to do with planning and understanding your [budget] numbers, and understanding clearly what you wish to do in the year of the budget …
>
> The first issue around departments when we talk about planning [is the case of continuous shifting of funds]. As a department, you must be in a position to ensure that you do the things that you said you would do. Not going on changing [because of poor planning].
>
> Our department continues with efforts aimed at improving the alignment of strategic plans with budgets, as well as the monitoring, evaluation and reporting of budget information.

In the context of the large shifts in expenditure commented on earlier, the general impression created in these interviews is that such re-prioritisation of expenditure would not have been possible if provinces alone were tasked with ensuring allocative efficiency at such a large scale. Hence, decisions taken outside of provincial governments, especially at intergovernmental fora, appear to be the most decisive places where such changes were driven.

## Provincial budgeting, budget practices and allocative efficiency

Provincial respondents (both treasuries and the two service delivery departments) raised a number of issues that have, in our view, a direct impact on the ability of provinces to deploy resources to where they are needed the most. The issues mentioned contain factors that enhance and retard allocative efficiency at the provincial level. The most relevant factors discussed were:

- the limited revenue-raising ability of provinces;

- the continuation of unfunded mandates, especially in the social services sector;

- incremental budget practices that have little connection with strategic-level planning and budgeting;

- a general climate of economic uncertainty, forcing spending cuts and mandating re-prioritisation;

- 'confusion' around the assignment of expenditure functions and how this limits the ability of provinces to spend on issues they have identified;

- the complete absence of civil society organisations (CSOs) in allocation debates and decisions at the provincial level; and

- the role of intergovernmental fora in deciding provincial priorities.

It is a well-known fact and consequence of our constitutional dispensation that provincial governments do not have sufficient revenue sources. Presently, own revenue comprises approximately 3% on average of total provincial revenue, the so-called 'unconditional' block grant 78%, while earmarked funding (conditional grants) comprises 19% on average of total provincial revenue.[iv] Provincial own revenue, as a share of total provincial revenue, ranges from 1.2% in the Eastern Cape to 5% in the Western Cape. Thus, even among provincial governments, there are differential discretionary spending margins. Also, a significant part of provincial resources deals with expenditure on compensation, which is nationally set and nationally bargained. It requires very little imagination to realise that, unless provinces are allowed to exploit own revenue sources or show more efficiency in collecting what is due to them, they will continue to struggle with diminished fiscal scope, thus further questioning their ability to effect provincial processes and realities.

Although unfunded provincial mandates are no longer the curse they used to be (see Barberton, 2002), they affect materially the perception and reality of fiscal space for provincial governments. It would also be fair to say that both national departments and provincial governments have made inroads into eradicating incremental budgeting practices, but some respondents insisted that this remains a reality. By not connecting spending to policy or the emerging needs of the province, incremental budget practices would obviously be a threat to provincial allocative efficiency. However, the spending evidence reviewed earlier suggests that material spending shifts have taken place. It is becoming increasingly clear that such shifts were not engineered by provincial governments and appear to reflect extant intergovernmental fiscal practice.

The remaining three issues (economic uncertainty, the importance of intergovernmental fora, and role confusion) are just as important in determining the magnitude of the fiscal space available to provincial governments. While global economic growth is outside of the immediate control of the government, function and expenditure assignment across the three spheres of government is relatively clear in South Africa (Barberton, 2002), and interdependent governance is the cornerstone of modern democratic South Africa. Below are reflections by respondents on some of these issues.

---

*Box 2*

In addition, although the MTEF budgeting framework was meant to create higher levels of stability and to improve forward planning, too much uncertainty still exists regarding the allocations of future years. This was especially relevant over the past three financial years as well as the current 2010 MTEF process due to the negative economic environment that results in substantial budget cuts and the need for re-prioritisation.

We've got a thing called the 10-by-10, which is the nine provincial treasuries, the nine provincial education departments and the two national departments [treasury and education]. They agree jointly on a set of priorities for the sector, which is similar to the old Function Committee system. So you agree, these are the main priorities for education, health, social development, housing, transport, etc.

---

However, while interdependent government and governance is mandated constitutionally, and given the weaknesses at provincial level in deploying resources where they are most needed, and accounting for the reality of large spending shifts, the second respondent in Box 2 sums up well how we got to where we are today. Intergovernmental fora have simply taken the place of the Function Committees that existed prior to 1997/98 and are, in fact, the most decisive places where resource allocation decisions are made. Thus, for our overall allocative efficiency picture, it does not matter that provinces are technically weak, but for provincial governments intent on influencing provincial outcomes, this reality is devastating and questions the true role and import of provincial governments. The oft-repeated saying that provincial governments have been turned into provincial administrations finds powerful support in this account of allocative efficiency and it remains questionable whether provinces will contribute to future debates on where scarce government resources should be spent.

## Political interference in the budget process and allocative efficiency

The budget process in South Africa is designed to give political input an important role in the final allocation decisions. The government's strategic medium-term frameworks serve as an example of how political content conditions policies and the resource allocation process. However, it is assumed, outside of natural and social disasters, that unregulated inputs and demands could derail spending plans and affect the extent to which provincial governments are able to protect policy-vital spending.

Respondents across provincial and national government levels made it clear that political interference remains an issue that upsets careful planning and destroys good budget practices. Box 3 offers examples of some of the strong sentiments that have been expressed by respondents.

---

**Box 3**

Our government here decides they are going to have what we call a flagship project. But this is done when these decisions are taken well outside of the budgeting process and they then decide what they are going to do and where the funds would come from. And as a result, somebody comes up with a clever idea that they should take 1% from every department's budget. And then you find that it means that now the plans of departments are almost derailed.

These challenges [high turnover of senior personnel] were common to national and provincial departments, and the most significant challenges that were experienced include ... budgets were poorly compiled, hence making implementation difficult, and there was evidence of political interference in the in-year implementation of budgets.

Our department continues with efforts aimed at improving the alignment of strategic plans with budgets, as well as the monitoring, evaluation and reporting of budget information.

---

It is difficult to establish objectively the magnitude of this problem at national and provincial level,[v] but whatever the sums of money involved, this kind of interference would further undermine the ability of provincial governments to link strategic plans and budgets. Planned and policy-driven allocation of resources is vulnerable in this political scheme. But in a strange and perverse way, such forceful and direct political intervention does make the case for the importance of spending on provincial realities, even though it heightens the State's vulnerability to corruption and unethical practices.

# Operational efficiency

How does the PFMA conceive of operational matters and ensure that a performance element is brought into the management of public resources? Firstly, it does this through the responsibilities of the AO and especially section 38(b): '[The accounting officer] is responsible for the effective, efficient, economical and transparent use of the resources of the department, trading entity or constitutional institution.'

This responsibility is also extended to other officials in the employ of a government department, trading entity or constitutional institution (section 45(b)). Secondly, section 27(4) of the legislation ensures that the way in which budgets are presented to Parliament allows the latter and the broader public to exercise oversight by specifying that each programme should have measurable objectives.

Thirdly, various reporting requirements specified in terms of the legislation allow feedback to politicians and the broader public about the results achieved using public resources. These reports include the departmental Annual Report (sections 40(1)(d) and 40(3)(a), and the quarterly financial and service delivery reports from provincial governments (section 32(2)).

Fourthly, under the general responsibilities of AOs, section 38(1)(a)(iii) requires that the AO puts into being and maintains 'an appropriate procurement and provisioning system which is fair, equitable, transparent, competitive and cost-effective'. This is obviously very important from a performance point of view, because tenders that have been awarded to the wrong persons and businesses are doubly costly and inefficient for the government. In the latest Report of the Auditor General (2011), which examines the performance of provincial education and health departments on their infrastructure projects, it is indicated that the costs of replacement contractors amount to approximately R64 million for education and R537 million for health. These contractors are brought in because tenders were awarded to the wrong persons and companies, or to persons and companies that have multiple contracts with government, resulting in inefficiencies in the way tenders are managed.

The abovementioned provisions in the PFMA are aimed at providing enough information to policy makers, politicians in Parliament and the broader public about how well resources are translated into results. One expects, therefore, that such information is useful to departments internally as they seek to improve their performance. This presupposes that departments have systems in place that allow them to identify useful information, review this information and use it as a basis for informing final allocations to functions and programmes.

Folscher and Cole (2006:31) provide a compelling description of the state of public finance reform when they argue that:

'All in all, the South African system has reformed fast, up to a point, but has been struggling to deepen the reforms in order to further enhance service delivery. It can be argued that whereas fiscal discipline has been achieved, and the allocation of scarce resources to spending priorities improved, addressing efficiency issues *is the greatest challenge remaining* [author emphasis]. Perhaps in these areas it is not only the public financial management systems that are at fault, but further reforms need to be co-ordinated with improvements in parallel systems, such as human resources management.'

This quote is useful for two reasons: one, it summarises well the consensus position on the achievements of our public finance reforms, including the implementation of the PFMA; and two, the authors suggest that inchoate systems developed under the PFMA are part of the reason for the dire performance of government institutions in improving the lives of ordinary South Africans. This position is not universally accepted as had become clear from interviewing national and provincial respondents.

In the next sections, we identify key dimensions of the operational efficiency equation as seen through the eyes of national and provincial government practitioners. We supplement this reflection and discussion by using academic research and official government data on the various aspects addressed in this sub-section. The following factors were consistently identified by respondents as having a significant bearing on the implementation of the PFMA and government departments' overall efficiency:

- capacity constraints and skills shortages;
- variable AO performance and poor use of disciplinary and criminal provisions in the Act;
- negative impact of politicians on implementation;
- compliance burden of legislation (public finance, human resources and sectoral legislation);
- lack of proper back-up implementation and administrative systems; and
- the overall usefulness of capacity development.

## Capacity constraints, skills shortages and operational efficiency

Capacity constraints and skills shortages had a significant impact on the (phased) implementation of the PFMA, especially its operational efficiency dimensions. In our correspondence with the National Treasury, it was indicated that, because measurable objectives were 'new concepts in the public finance arena', implementation of this (performance) aspect of the PFMA was delayed for implementation until 2002. While the postponement made sense from an operational and readiness point of view, it conveys powerfully how the operational aspects of the PFMA took a backseat at the onset of the legislation's implementation. Respondents reflected on this matter in the following ways:

---

**Box 4**

[Capacity is lacking in the areas of] asset management, what else, internal control. What we mean by internal controls? We want actual inspectorates where the link between the hospitals and the head office – where you can check whether the PFMA has been implemented – is sufficient. Currently, we have capacity in head office, but you don't have capacity to also check that the hospitals and other institutions are doing it.

OK, I think in almost everything that you have mentioned, with us for instance, its capacity, the segregation of duties as indicated in the PFMA. For example, in the hospitals, due to shortage of financial staff in the hospital, there are only one or two people who must do procurement payment, whereas the PFMA clearly states there must be segregation of duties.

However, there are issues of capacity. The issues of skills – which are coming out – are not really sufficient to enable 100% compliance with the PFMA. The [public finance] skills are not always sufficient. But we cannot sit here in treasury and do the budget for a department that has its own accountability system. But really, in terms of planning and linking your things to the budget and your plan, it has been difficult.

---

Although the first comment refers to the health sector, one can generalise this pronouncement to other sectors, especially where service delivery sites are decentralised. In provincial education, large sums of money are transferred to schools to pay for textbooks, small capital equipment and municipal services, and follow-up transfer payments are conditional upon schools providing financial statements. Due to the large number of schools, provincial education departments are unable to verify the veracity and quality of all the financial reports, thus leaving the door open to the inefficient and corrupt use of government resources.[vi] Some provincial education departments make use of management consultant companies, but, invariably, even these private service-providers will audit and assess a sample of schools only. One has to assume that departments' inability to verify the veracity and quality of financial reports of extra-budgetary institutions has a negative effect on the resources-outcomes link and, hence, operational efficiency is jeopardised.

The second quote also speaks to the issue of the segregation of duties and, in this regard, Folscher and Cole (2006:21) state that checks and balances have been instituted to ensure that individuals undertake their duties. They provide an example of payroll systems where the person tasked with establishing the legitimacy of payments is different from the person making the actual payments. This minimises the possibility of collusion and corruption, thereby ensuring that, at the first hurdle, resources are put to use as per departmental requirements and planning. Failure to do so represents severe risks for departments and puts effective and efficient service delivery in jeopardy. Capacity constraints and skilled staff shortages do not, therefore, only affect planning and strategic deployment of resources, but are also directly implicated in the poor state of service delivery in South Africa. The situation that the respondents reflect upon does not necessarily imply broken systems, but merely says that staff shortages compromise the full operational implementation of the PFMA.

Due to the undeveloped nature of the operational efficiency dimensions of the PFMA, very little objective data exist that measure this aspect of the legislation. In personal communication with Mr Jayce Nair from National Treasury, he intimated that the National Treasury 'recently developed a Financial Management Capability Maturity Model (FMCMM) to assess the financial maturity of PFMA-compliant institutions. Since using this tool, it is quite clear that [we are] still in the developmental stages and still need to progress to the point where it can be determined whether public funds are being spent in accordance with the three e's (economy, efficiency and effectiveness). The FMCMM has been designed with six different levels, with the first three focusing on compliance and controls. Levels 4, 5 and 6 will focus on the three e's and, amongst others, how well money has been spent. We anticipate assessing departments in this regard sometime during the 2012/2013 financial year.'

There are two points that need to be emphasised from this statement: one, most public institutions are focused on complying with the legislation and any advanced engagement with the three e's of the PFMA is still some way off; and two, although the result of the capability assessment is an average score for a department, scores are averaged across functions (asset management, liability management, compensation of employees, etc.), which are populated by persons, thus the question of capacity and skills are implied in these assessments. The generally low scores on this diagnostic tool across national and provincial departments are, in part, a reflection of the poor skills set in the public sector. This is also a clear statement about how the lack of skills in the public sector is preventing advanced engagement with and implementation of the PFMA.

## Variable AO performance and operational efficiency

The PFMA vests a lot of authority in AOs and makes these officials responsible for the effective and efficient management of resources in government departments. The extent to which government departments reach their policy and service delivery goals is a direct function of the professional calibre of the AO.

In a piece that deals with capacity building in African public servants, Obadan (2005) notes that economic and financial management skills need to be appreciated against the background of public sector reform. Public sector reform must have one overarching goal and, according to Obadan, this is the development of a critical mass of expertise to analyse, articulate and implement development policies, programmes and projects in various sectors. Ajam (2007), in reference to the role of the Chief Financial Officer (CFO), makes the point that such officials should know enough of the core technical aspects of service delivery in order to be effective. These remarks are equally applicable to the position of the AO. Kusi (2006) notes that getting civil servants to manage for results and transforming State agencies into active producers of public services has taken more time than anticipated. Maphiri (2011) describes an extensive process of in-year management and monitoring, which requires high-quality leadership and management control to achieve integrated public finance management.

This shortlist of desirable skills for senior managers is far from exhaustive, but already looks daunting. How are AOs seen by their colleagues in national and provincial treasuries, as well as provincial and national service delivery departments? And what do these perceptions tell us about the state of leadership at this level? Finally, how does weak leadership affect the achievement of operational efficiency? Below, we provide a sample of some of the comments from respondents.

*Box 5*

You'd find departments that are very good. And you also find departments that are not so good. As a result, we are putting more and more emphasis on developing financial management skills in various areas. So within the province [there are departments] that did not under- or over-spend and getting a clean report. But you find others with huge over-spent budgets, poor financial management, disclaimer audit reports ...

[The performance of accounting officers] has not improved. It has worsened. It differs you see. In 2005, we had only about two departments with qualifications. 2006, I don't remember 2006, but 2007 we had more than two. From one year to the next, you never know what is going to happen. At best, we have not improved.

In general, the performance of accounting officers for the period 2000 to 2008 can be described as good. However, improvements can still be made towards improving the quality of the annual financial statements, annual reports, monthly reports, etc. Our department therefore interacts regularly with clients with a view to providing assistance to improve their financial management.

Comments from the first two respondents reflect on differences within the same locality and differences across time. The latter reflects a perennial problem that has plagued senior financial management, namely the incessant turnover and movement of scarce-skills staff members. This obviously brings with it instability and changing public finance fortunes in service delivery departments. One would have to assume that service delivery would be affected, because a department whose finances are mismanaged can hardly be thought to deliver high-quality services to its primary recipients. Differences in financial leadership within provinces could possibly reflect that some departments offer better working conditions or have generally more skilled staff, but this raises the question of just how united the public-service cadres are within a province. And how does a provincial treasury, the provincial government per se, let some departments' performance slip so badly?

A further context to the variable performance of AOs is the oft-repeated assertion by respondents that mismanagement and wrongdoing are left unpunished within departments. Some respondents felt that what weakens the implementation of the PFMA and, by extension, operational effectiveness, are unjustified feelings among government officials that no action will be taken. What does the financial misconduct of national and provincial department look like? The PSC publishes annually a review of financial misconduct cases.[vii] Figure 4 shows the number of reported cases for the period 2001/02 to 2008/09.

**Figure 4: Number of reported financial misconduct cases and percentage of employees found guilty, 2001/02 to 2008/09**

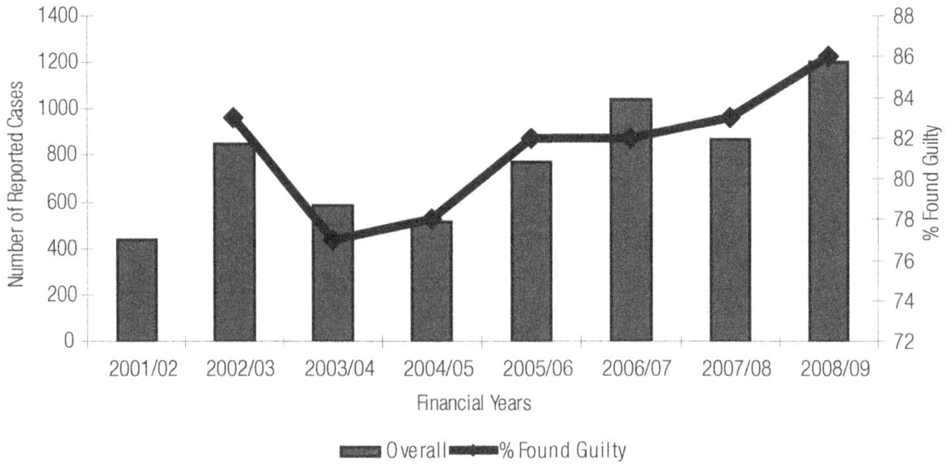

*Source: Based on PSC data (2010:10)*

The data in Figure 4 suggest that action is taken in instances where there is financial misconduct. The number of reported cases in 2008/09 was 1 204, of which 86% returned guilty verdicts. In fact, throughout the data series, it appears as soon as a person is charged with financial misconduct, there is a very high chance that he or she will be found guilty. The percentage of employees found guilty ranges from 77% in 2003/04 to 86% in 2008/09. We are, of course, also interested in the percentage of senior managers that are implicated in financial misconduct. The data from the PSC suggest that 4.5% of reported cases in 2004/05 and 1.9% of reported cases in 2008/09 involved senior managers.

To further investigate (or validate) the complaints by respondents that little action is taken when financial misconduct takes place, we next examine the kind of punishment that was imposed on guilty public servants. Figure 5 provides information on the kind of sanctions imposed on affected State employees for the period 2002/03 to 2008/09.

Initially, a rather large percentage of cases resulted in formal discharge from the public service. In 2002/03, 47% (225 cases) of those investigated for financial misconduct were discharged, but this figure fell to 11% in 2008/09. An increasing number of guilty employees receive a final written warning as a disciplinary step, while 23% receive a combination of sanctions. If our conclusions were to be based on this data alone, then clearly some tough action has been taken against guilty government employees, thus implying that the respondents in our interviews exaggerated the 'toothless' nature of the PFMA and associated public-service regulations.

**Figure 5: Main forms of sanctions imposed during the period 2002/03 to 2008/09**

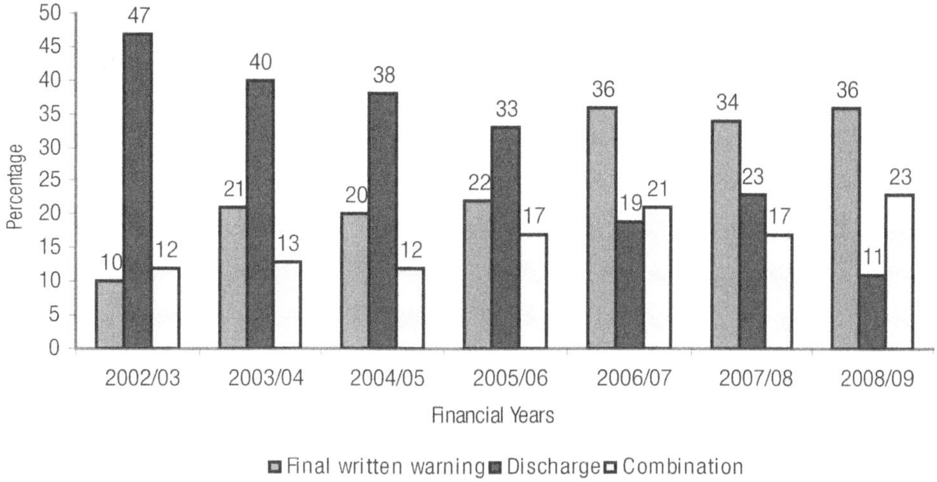

☐ Final written warning ■ Discharge ☐ Combination

*Source: PSC (2010:12)*

However, the absolute number of reported cases for State employees generally and for senior managers more specifically appear quite small given the size of the public service sector. It could be that these cases are only the tip of the iceberg and that there is indeed an unwillingness to bring all offenders to book. In its reflection on provincial auditing outcomes for the 2009/10 financial year, the Auditor-General report (2010:18) states that cases of financial misconduct are indicators that internal controls are not working as they should, or, alternatively, these internal controls are overridden. The best we can conclude on this matter is that there is evidence of strong action and there is no reason why this would not be continued. However, the absolute numbers leave us unsure whether all financial misconduct is measured comprehensively by the available data. The delivery agreement for Outcome 12 supports the views of respondents on the reluctance of managers to take action against staff members who transgress public-service provisions. The delivery agreement states that it takes several months for disciplinary processes to be started and that there are significant inconsistencies in the type of sanction applied (Department of Public Services and Administration, 2010).

Despite the rather gloomy picture of the state of financial management at the highest government levels, it is important to note that the National Treasury recognised public finance management skills gaps as an important issue and instituted a series of conditional grants aimed at improving public level financial management skills. One such example is the education sector, where the quality improvement and financial management grant was awarded to provincial education departments to strengthen their financial management capacity. In his Report to the President of South Africa on the state of education in 2002, Minister of Education, Professor Kader Asmal, argued that improvements took place through better systems for planning and monitoring, but cautioned that more work was needed on improving procurement systems. Other departments that benefited from financial management capacity grants were health, social welfare and the then State expenditure department (National Treasury, 2000).

## The 'compliance burden' and operational efficiency

Are provincial treasuries and, more specifically, service delivery departments, subjected to reporting requirements that detract from the job of delivering public services? The interview data has provided interesting perspectives on this issue and is summarised thus:

- There is a difference in reporting requirements for treasuries and for service delivery departments. The former are subjected to the PFMA and the Public Service Act, 1994 (No. 103 of 1994), while the latter add further sectoral-specific legislation to the list of constitutional and legal matters that must be observed and responded to. In that sense, there is a differential reporting burden.

- In our written exchange with the National Treasury, they made it clear that such complaints were received from provincial political heads (Premiers), but that the latter had not produced convincing evidence to prove that compliance reporting is indeed the order of the day or that provincial AOs find these requirements onerous.

- However, while the National Treasury flatly denies that the reporting requirements are onerous, the point was made that there are still large quality differences in the ability of reporting entities to submit reports of an acceptable standard. While we have established capacity differences as a potential explanation for this state of affairs, it is hard to rule out a compliance mentality, especially given the legal consequences (at least on paper, as we also showed) of transgressing provisions of the PFMA.

- Some respondents have pointed out that the onerous reporting require- ments are made doubly difficult by the uncoordinated information requests that emanate from the National Treasury. We have not been able to verify this allegation with the National Treasury and, therefore, cannot assess the validity of this interpretation.

More research is needed on the matter because, if a compliance men- tality exists, the quality of service delivery and operational effectiveness information is compromised. In fact, there is widespread acceptance that the quality of the annual and quarterly service delivery reports is variable and, hence, less useful for an analysis of service delivery trends.

The answer does not lie in reducing the information that is now avail- able to Parliament and the public at large, but to ensure that the informa- tion is not misleading and actually provides an accurate assessment of the state of service delivery. Hence, concerns about the existence of a compli- ance mentality cannot and should not be solved by reducing the quantity and quality of service delivery information at our disposal.

# Dashboard summary of three budget outcomes

| Table 2: Summary of implementation factors and their impact on the present budget outcomes | | |
| --- | --- | --- |
| Budget outcomes | Implementation factors | Impact of implementation factors |
| Aggregate fiscal discipline | Introduction of the MTEF budget framework | Hard ceilings discipline spending claims on the fiscus; top-down nature of the budget process reduces departmental 'budget games'; discussion of 'options' during budget pro-cess focuses departmental thinking on available resources |
| | Consensus-building in intergovernmental fora | Domination of African National Congress (ANC) provincial governments eases target-setting and agreeing to fiscal targets; finance MINMEC (Budget Council) is an influential body driven by consensus-building and fiscal results |
| | Political backing pro-vided to finance ministry | Internal and external pressures to increase spending beyond targets successfully resisted through the backing of National Treasury by political leadership in government |

| Allocative efficiency | Poor level of planning and strategic skills at provincial level | Spending on unplanned shortfalls; hastily put-together political priorities that add further pressure on spending; moving around of resources to fill unplanned gaps reduce departmental effectiveness in moving resources to where they are needed |
| --- | --- | --- |
| | Revenue allocation process that hamstring provincial discretionary spending | Limited fiscal space and poor planning skills make it less likely that provincial departments develop medium- and long-term plans that address provincial needs and priorities |
| | Importance of intergovernmental fora | Politicians have used such fora to great effect for their respective sectors, especially those that include sector and finance politicians; policies that are considered important, but are poorly funded, can be discussed and guarantees provided for better funding |
| Operational efficiency | Dedicated and thoughtful capacity building and support by the National Treasury | Given the low levels of skills in public service, National Treasury involvement in financial management is pivotal for the earlier successes around compliance, especially their template-driven interventions |
| | Human resources capacity constraints | The financial capability instrument confirms that we are at the compliance stage and that existing personnel place limitations on how fast the system can progress to advanced financial management for outcomes |
| | Insular departments at national and provincial levels | Inability of departments to use external data (AG reports, the public, portfolio committees) means they are unable to change the service delivery mechanism to make them more efficient and results-driven |
| | Lack of measurement of efficiency | Prior to the introduction of the financial capability framework, departments had no target or benchmark to strive for and AG audits are insufficient to determine the financial management level of departments |

# A closer look at implementation successes and challenges

A remarkable feature of the implementation of the PFMA has been the strong capacity building that took place both prior to and during the implementation of the Act. The National Treasury played a substantial role in making sure that new proposals were properly understood, and involved both national departments and provincial governments in such efforts. All the provincial respondents affirmed that capacity building was consistently done across the various stages of implementing the PFMA. Also, provincial treasuries, provincial departments and national departments were involved in the extensive training and capacity-building events.

Our proposition is that capacity building has been central to the implementation successes witnessed over the last ten years. What we do not know is how capacity building is linked to implementation successes and whether the secondary literature or the interview data will help us to better understand its role. We also explore what we consider to be the limits of the National Treasury capacity-building model and we try and link that directly to some of the implementation challenges that still plague our public finance system. While respondents have provided an array of implementation successes and challenges, for the purposes of this discussion we have focused on factors that appear to be common in the responses of the national and provincial respondents.

## Implementation successes

From an analysis of the secondary literature and the interviews with treasuries and service delivery departments, we came to the conclusion that there are two distinct implementation successes for which little or no evidence to the contrary exists. Of course, other authors have provided evidence of different kinds of successes, but our ploy here was to select only those successes over which there are no serious and fundamental disagreements.[viii]

One, the PFMA has fundamentally altered the overall reporting and budget information environment in the public service. Although there are questions about the overall quality of such reports and disputes over whether the reporting burden is disproportionate, it is near impossible to resist the proposition that the PFMA generated more budget information (financial and non-financial), which is now freely available to parliamentarians and the broader public. Not only is more information available, but such information is also provided timely as per the implementation schedules laid out in the PFMA. This transpired in spite of initial fears that the implementation schedules for submission of financial and consolidated reports are too punishing.

Respondents' assessment of this proposition is reproduced below and, because it is such a central part of the text, we have quoted at length (in some instances the verbal stream was rearranged to extract the overall meaning of the response).

---

*Box 6*

External independent bodies are also of the view that the PFMA has contributed towards the improvement of financial management in the public sector. This view was expressed by the Auditor-General whilst the South African Institute of Government Auditors is of the view that the quality of public sector annual reports exceeds the quality of the private sector annual reports, especially with regards to the amount of pertinent information that is provided.

So the PFMA brought a non-financial performance management [aspect] that wasn't there in the old Exchequer's Act. So that by itself was a quantum leap into the future. However, it took about six years really to get into ... the system. So this is probably the first year [2010] I think that we would be able to test whether ... how well we have done with performance management and linking them into the way the budget is done.

Since we started to table this Budget Statement, I mean it has a lot of information and so does the Budget Speech at provincial level. The legislature is filled to capacity. Because now we are saying with the state of the province address ... information is coming out. And that we also have radios now. I mean the FM is based here in the city at one of the SABC radio stations. But the question is now ... are we really touching the lives of the poor out there?

I think the biggest success, I think here is that you start reporting on annual financial statements and making disclosures. Whereas in the past it was a one page appropria-tion account, full stop! You are following things up now. Your ... over-expenditure, or let's call it unauthorised expenditure under the old appropriations account, I mean so what? Your accounting procedures now stay until it's approved. It can't disappear. I think those [non-financial information requirements] are very good information management to make government's spending more transparent.

---

The third quote reveals a very interesting dimension to the new infor-mation-rich environment under the PFMA: communities and citizens demand to know more about how government resources are likely to affect their lives. While the respondent's views in the second quote also touches on the importance of non-financial information, none of the respondents believed we had made enough progress in integrating financial and non-financial information. The fourth quote reveals how someone who was familiar with public finance management under the old Exchequer Act system appreciates the new sense of accountability that has been intro-duced with the superior reporting requirements of the PFMA. Generally, even respondents who are very critical about the overall contribution of the PFMA to solving service delivery crises admit that the information environment under the Act has been changed irrevocably for the better.

Two, the PFMA and associated regulations have undoubtedly contrib-uted to improved transparency in the budget information that is available and presented in official government documents. External and objective evidence for this is our comparative standing among both developed and developing countries as measured by the OBI.[ix] In the 2010 version, South Africa was ranked the most open and transparent provider of budget information, making this information widely available to the media and the public in general, and producing national budget documentation of outstanding quality.

The question remains as to why the PFMA has been so successful in generating more (and in some instances better) information and contributing to improved transparency. We believe that capacity building that leads to the production of templates (or toolkits) and the availability of sufficient and clear guidelines that assist officials in the completion of various annual budget reports (proposals and implementation) might be one of the reasons for the success in producing reports on time. This does not gainsay the systems that support the production of financial and non-financial information, but, as we suggest in the next section, evidence is strong that such systems are not optimal, do not speak to each other, and in some instances (M&E, for example), systems are not yet in place. What we are saying is that capacity building that has concrete reference points has a better chance of altering behaviour. Logically, this implies that any task in the legislation that cannot be executed by means of a checklist approach, and which relies on individual skills and discretion, is likely to be harder, more challenging, and government's capacity-building efforts in making officials legislation-compliant will prove to be less effective.

However, a powerful rival explanation is that producing information on time is the raison d'être for public finance legislation per se, and that any delays would destroy the entire system of accountability within and outside of the Executive branch of government. Hence, information generation was given the highest priority by the Executive, entirely in keeping with the phased implementation of the PFMA. Over time, we should see steady gains in areas that appear intractable as policy and implementation attention shifts away from generating information to guaranteeing quality information and meaningful service delivery outcomes. This sounds entirely plausible, but we feel there is good reason to believe that the success of capacity building in the context of the PFMA is limited to specific areas and that not all aspects of the Act lend themselves to the template-driven capacity-building approach.

# Implementation challenges

The ultimate implementation standard by which service delivery and public finance management should be measured remains those provisions of the PFMA that require an emphasis on economy, effectiveness, efficiency and transparency in the use of government resources.

But what does this mean? Superficially, it seems to imply that services delivered should become cheaper as they improve; government must deliver the right mix of services (quantity and quality) to primary beneficiaries, devise systems that transparently show how resources have been used, and report what results and outcomes have been bought with public resources. This, by any service delivery standard, is a tall order and requires officials who understand the policy and service delivery context and within the limitations of the resources envelope of the spending unit, to deliver services as per the PFMA prescriptions. Hence, a key aspect of this process is an iterative refinement of service delivery mechanisms and the ability to measure how well spending units perform their assigned service delivery and spending mandates.

One implementation challenge relates to the inability of departments to establish a coherent and comprehensive M&E system. Commentators routinely refer to the poor quality of the indicators, their arbitrariness, and the fact that these indicators do not meaningfully measure the service in question. Respondents' take on this matter is reproduced below, but in a real way, meaningful quality indicators can only be developed in the context of a comprehensive M&E system that captures key policy and service delivery information.

---

*Box 7*

When the PFMA was implemented, the non-financial [bit] has not been implemented together. *Because national [treasury] must give you guidelines and formats how to do that.* And they only started currently last year. They are still busy developing this kind of reporting format for non-financial information. The people must still be trained how to use the non-financial [information] in league [in conjunction] with the financial. The PFMA there does not give guidance there.

I mean I will say that's still a new thing for me [non-financial information] growing up like a small child. You will find that you have this non-financial information in the budget, in the annual plans of the department. But if you say you want to build a school and so many schools, I think ... as you go to the annual reports, you must talk about the same information. To say, I set myself a target of building three schools and then you should be able to find that information at the end [in the annual reports]. It's not the same [the information reported and the target do not speak to each other].

Since the National Treasury issued the 'Framework for Managing Programme Performance Information', the quality of performance information in strategic plans and annual reports has improved significantly. The Framework provides a greater understanding of key concepts relating to performance measurement. Performance indicators, targets and measurable objectives continue to improve on an annual basis.

Feedback from quotes one and three reinforce the point we made earlier around the need for guided assistance (read templates) for national and provincial officials in the implementation of the PFMA. These respondents make it clear that since the National Treasury provided direct assistance and guidance, improvements in the quality of indicators followed. This evidence supports our proposition that capacity building by treasuries (and National Treasury mostly) is most successful when the outcome is a concrete product or template that can be used 'as is' for departmental purposes. Given the decentralised intentions of the PFMA and the need for managers to 'manage', it is worrying that success in the implementation of the PFMA can only be claimed when there is direct intervention by the National Treasury. Complicated tasks such as designing service delivery interventions that are effective, efficient, economical and transparent cannot be managed as per the template capacity-building approach. And given the second respondent's concern that adopted indicators are not necessarily the ones that are reported on, the implementation of the PFMA appears destined to run into serious problems unless innovative and resourceful senior managers are in bountiful supply.

An important consequence of the effective, efficient, economical and transparent use of government resources is the need to learn iteratively (using financial and non-financial data) about what works and what does not. By not having fully-fledged M&E systems, departments risk not learning from implementation and their service delivery mistakes. This brings us to our second implementation challenge: the frequency and rate at which departments respond to recommendations made to them by the AG. There appears to be a broken chain between the recommendations of the AG, the actions and discussions in the various public accounts committees in Parliament and provincial legislatures, and the remedial actions that should happen in affected departments. As one respondent put it: 'But you see, it [compliance with AG findings] differs in departments. There are those I know, they don't worry. As we are speaking, I have just received a management letter for 2008/09. You are not going to get anything here that says this issue was raised last year. Because I act on them.'

This respondent appears to be one of the good officials who respond immediately to concerns raised by the AG, but implies that this responsiveness is not a feature of the government department in which he or she is employed. This was asserted by many of the respondents, who said that new staff often has to deal with AG recommendations that they know nothing about. This leads to lethargic responses and, in many instances, the same departments get the same qualified audits or disclaimers. For our purposes, and the fact that we speak about an iterative service delivery approach, this suggests again that many government departments are not prepared to learn and to remedy where appropriate. There are departments operating without proper M&E systems and follow-up, and no remedial action is taken on AG recommendations. The broader picture that emerges is one of insularity. Without this iterative learning process, it is hard to conceive of services being implemented that are increasingly cheaper, better and more focused, and where results are reviewed and used in formulating new service delivery strategies.

The third implementation challenge we want to highlight is the extraordinary reality where citizens and civil society as a whole are not involved in allocation decisions or consulted on operational matters. Here are some respondents' comments on citizens' involvement in the budget process:

---

**Box 8**

I think the problem we have is because we are running at a very tight deadline. We will produce the documentation that we need to provide because I mean it is an enormous database that we have to put together. And that's usually finished just in time for printing and then it's a week before you need to table the stuff. But their [civil society's] request for gender budgets and children's budgets, I mean – I can say guys, that's the information, use the books. So if Idasa wants to come and say, there's the book, you can do something for civil society. But by that time, we are done with budgets.

There is supposed to be consultation every time we go and present our budget proposals in terms of the appropriations bill. Now the requirement is that this bill must then to be taken to the people for their comments. I have been here since 2005 – I have never heard at any one time that no, we must change that allocation on health because members of the society, they are saying one, two and three, etc. I really think it is an act of complying [taking the budget to the people], but I really doubt whether it is helping ...

I really don't know what the public get out of it, but from a management point of view, there's quite a lot of things that you now learn that you did not know in the past. Whether the public really look at it, I don't know. Maybe a few interested people. But I really don't know ... at the end of the day, it's very difficult to measure.

---

The last two respondents appear to reflect on a symbolic procedure that does not seem to have any real impact. This represents provincial treasuries as going through the motions, but not getting substantial feedback, or, even if they do, not using it to make any changes to the proposed budget allocations. The first respondent seems to be saying that the timeframe of the budget process is so squeezed that there is insufficient time to consult, and that working with citizens and civil society is best left to NGO practitioners. This view was shared by two other provincial treasuries for whom the concept of consulting with citizens is alien and unproductive.

Although the issue of citizen participation seems to be removed from the first two implementation challenges (the absence of M&E systems and variable follow-up on AG recommendations), it falls into the same category of problem for departments. Not engaging with citizens and communities means that the ultimate beneficiaries of government services do not have a say in how such services could be improved. This leaves departments even more insular and unable to respond to emerging challenges in communities. However, we are sympathetic to the plight of provincial treasuries because of time constraints and a bureaucratic culture that is inimical to citizen participation. Provincial-level participation is probably not the most strategic place to start engaging the idea of participatory budgets, but maybe provinces can help facilitate such discussions.

We feel that these three implementation challenges of the PFMA are serious – although not the only ones, of course – because they suggest points of breakdown and foregone learning opportunities. Government departments in the business of allocating resources and changing lives can ill-afford such insularity. The rising level of municipal protests (see Figure 6) is a clear warning that we need to reconsider the whole notion of civic participation and engagement in budgetary matters.

**Figure 6: Service-delivery protests by province, January 2004 to July 2011**

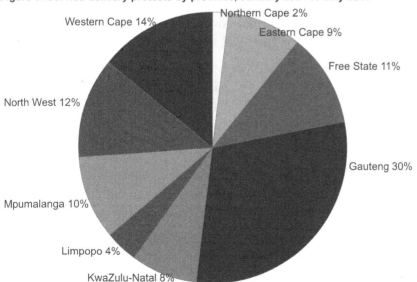

*Source: Municipal IQ: Municipal Hotspots Monitor, quoted in Department of Cooperative Governance, Research Weekly Alert, 5 August 2011.*

# Policy and legislative developments affecting the future implementation of the PFMA

Since the implementation of the PFMA in 2000, a number of new laws and policies were passed that have a direct bearing on financial management in South Africa. We focus on three developments in this section, namely the publication of delivery agreements for politicians; the passing of the Money Bills Amendment Procedure and Related Matters Act, No 9 of 2009; and recent trends towards performance auditing undertaken by the AG. All these developments have the potential to put into perspective some of the implementation successes and challenges that we have identified in the preceding paragraphs.

## Delivery agreements and potential impact on the implementation of the PFMA

The delivery agreement for Outcome 12 specifies a number of issues that the government needs to look into to improve the quality of financial management in the public service. Below, we provide what we believe are the most important dimensions of this strategy:

- Expenditure and cost reviews to determine if funds are correctly allocated and whether value for money is obtained with the approved spending resources;

- The development and implementation of a financial capability maturity tool to assess the various financial management functions undertaken by departments;

- An intense focus on reversing negative audit outcomes by synchronising the roles of officials and politicians, and strengthening both administrative and political accountability;

- The introduction of unit-cost methodologies to enhance the cost-effective implementation of government policies;

- The introduction of multi task teams to bolster measures aimed at preventing corruption in the supply-chain management process;

- Intensified financial management capacity-building across the three spheres of government, focused on both the individual and the organisation; and

- The introduction of a strategy to address staff shortages in the finance field.

While each recommendation requires detailed analysis to understand its potential impact on the implementation of the PFMA, we focus here on the introduction of expenditure reviews and unit-cost methodologies. Expenditure reviews have the potential to change the way departments look at spending on programmes and may achieve what the old activity-based budgeting proposals could not achieve. This has implications for where resources are spent (allocative efficiency) and what value for money can be achieved with alternative activities in programmes and sub-programmes.

The most innovative proposal, however, is the introduction of unit-cost methodologies. The idea of defining unit costs for the various services is a big step forward in determining whether we spend sufficient resources on certain activities, or whether we are spending more than we should. However, not having seen the unit-cost methodology, it is important that sector-specific details be scrutinised to ensure that activities and programmes are not deprived of valuable resources. From the point of view of the implementation of the PFMA, determining base levels of unit costs is essential to gauge whether departments are progressively providing services at a cheaper cost. This involves innovation in both the mechanisms chosen to deliver the service and a reduction in the underlying costs that define a service. If departments get this right, they should have access to important and realistic benchmarks, which could then be used in the service delivery improvement cycle. In the present situation, departments do not have access to this information and could, therefore, transition to targets blindly, which may be irrelevant and inaccurate.

## The Money Bills Amendment Procedure and Related Matters Act and its potential impact on the implementation of the PFMA

The Money Bills Amendment Procedure and Related Matters Act, 2009 (No 9 of 2009), is an important legislative contribution to the improved implementation of the PFMA. It does this by:

- Strengthening Parliament's engagement with strategic and budgetary documentation required in terms of the PFMA (quarterly service delivery reports, annual reports, etc.). If effective oversight is done, questions around the effective and efficient spending of resources could be explored in some detail by the relevant portfolio committees;

- Requiring the politicians in Parliament to take into account a set of principles when proposing amendments. These principles range from exhorting Parliament to accept fiscal prudence as an important part of their decision-making processes, and requiring parliamentarians to consider the service delivery implications (both in terms of obligation and improvements) of their proposed amendments. Hence, both aggregate fiscal discipline and operational efficiency considerations are taken into account in the formal amendment process;

- Considering the views of sector committees in the appropriation process by allowing a sector committee to advise the Appropriations Committee to appropriate resources conditionally, to ensure resources within a department/vote are spent effectively, efficiently and economically; and

- Establishing a Parliamentary Budget Office intended to provide politicians with an independent view on sector budgets, their implementation and the progress made in achieving policy goals. Provided this office is properly capacitated, it should strengthen political and legislative oversight, and make an important contribution to implementing the three e's of the PFMA.

## The trend towards performance auditing and its potential impact on the implementation of the PFMA

The AG's recent forays into the area of performance auditing have added a new dimension to performance management in government. This is to be welcomed and will support the fuller implementation of the PFMA. Some of the key trends that emerged in the 2009 and 2010 audit reports are outlined below.

- According to the 2010 and 2011 reports of the AG, executive oversight of the implementation of the budget is associated with positive audit outcomes and opinions. Practically, executive officers who call quarterly meetings to discuss progress in implementing the budget, review plans to strengthen the internal control environment, and inquire into progress in terms of responding to AG recommendations or SCOPA reports, are likely to head up departments that achieve clean audits. Theoretically, such departments have the basic public-finance ingredients to become all-out service delivery agents and realise the three e's of the PFMA.

- The AG made devastating findings on the availability, quality and consistency of non-financial information in departmental budget documents and reporting obligations. This included logical frameworks that do not make sense, the absence of supporting documentation to verify performance, and inadequate reporting on the deviation between planned and actual performance in departmental annual reports.

- Despite this gloomy picture, the AG makes the point that an increasing number of SCOPA recommendations are being implemented or in the process of being implemented. Obviously, there are still departments that respond to the recommendations in a tardy manner and, in some instances, no follow-up is being done. Departments that engage and implement the recommendations from the AG or SCOPA could break the cycle of insularity and use this information to improve their internal control environments, and, ultimately, their service delivery performance.

- Concerns over the supply-chain management process persist. In the 2011 audit report on infrastructure projects in provincial education and health departments, the AG made disconcerting findings on the Rand value of replacement contractors. This suggests that we are still not getting value for money from public spending on contractors and this has an immediate impact on the operational efficiency of departmental entities.

The present accountability and oversight environment provides fertile grounds for co-operation among Parliament, the AG and central government – National Treasury and the Department for Public Service and Administration (DPSA) – in the fuller implementation of the PFMA. It is a unique opportunity that should be exploited to the fullest, especially now that we are trying to make the transition from compliance to managing for results. A big part of the monitoring agenda of CSOs will be to establish whether such collaboration opportunities have been capitalised on, and whether this has resulted in better auditing and service delivery outcomes.

# Lessons learnt in the implementation of the PFMA in South Africa

South Africa is highly regarded for its achievements in the implementation of budget reforms and is often held up as a model for the region. Recent international successes, such as achieving first place in the OBI, further cement the unique leadership role that the country plays in the region. However, while there have been notable achievements, there are also a number of practices that should not be emulated by developing countries intent on similar budget-reform programmes. Below, we highlight some of the practices that could be encouraged in other contexts, as well as those practices that should be avoided.

## Practices to emulate in the implementation of framework public finance legislation and budget-reform measures

- Dedicated and thoughtful capacity-building interventions led by the National Treasury. The National Treasury realised early on that, in a public sector where skills are variable, implementation of the PFMA, if left entirely to sub-national governments, would produce very different results across jurisdictions, thus threatening the overall objectives of the PFMA. Through carefully devised templates, the National Treasury was able to guide the provision of information key to the legislative requirements of the PFMA. The best evidence of this capacity-building strategy can be seen in the submission of reporting documents that require some level of discretion in the way information is reported (for example, quarterly service delivery reports). The quality of information provided in these documents varies widely, as did the quality of non-financial information prior to the introduction of guided assistance to departments. While this strategy is obviously limited, it does explain to a large extent why departments were able to meet the legislative requirements of the PFMA in terms of the submission of budget documents and reports.

- Solid commitment to meeting the information and budget-reform targets as set out in the finance legislation and associated policies. Despite capacity challenges, the first ten years of the PFMA saw a proliferation of information and budget documents that were made available at the right time. To realise this vision, strong political and administrative leadership was required and the National Treasury provided such leadership. South Africa's elevation in the world of budget information and transparency is testimony to this commitment. A further part of this success recipe is, of course, the publication of Treasury Regulations, which provide practical guidance and clarity on the interpretation and implementation of the PFMA.

- The (late) introduction of the FMCMM measuring various levels of financial management competence. Although this instrument was introduced rather late in the implementation of the PFMA (in 2008), its addition is likely to have long-lasting impact. Prior to this, we could only rely on audit reports and, because such reports avoided performance issues, at most they provided a snapshot of the internal control environment within departmental entities. Now, because of the various levels of the tool, departments can be benchmarked, assessed annually, solid improvement and actions plans can be developed, and departments can work towards the realisation of these targets. Departments can identify specific areas where additional attention needs to be focused to get operating systems and personnel to work together. If properly implemented, this tool, by providing relevant information, could seriously move forward the fuller implementation of the PFMA.

- Fully functioning intergovernmental fora are needed to build consensus on the implementation of finance and sector legislation. There is little doubt that, in the absence of sector strategies, there is need for some form of collaboration between sector departments and their finance counterparts. New policy proposals that are being developed by say the education department could benefit from an intense engagement with finance authorities before the policy is published or perhaps even taken to Cabinet. In this paper, we have also produced evidence that suggests these fora were instrumental in effecting resource shifts at the provincial level. Our general take on this matter is that this was a useful strategy immediately after the end of apartheid, but, now that provinces are established, one expects these fora to be used for interventions other than deciding allocation decisions for provinces.

# Practices to avoid in the implementation of framework public finance legislation and budget-reform measures

- A comprehensive financial and budget-reform process that occurs rapidly, but without deepening reform gains. The first results of the FMCMM suggest that not all departments have achieved minimum levels of competence in the various disciplines of financial management. This does not refer to the more advanced aspects of financial management, but speaks to compliance with legislation and adherence to audit opinions. The recent audit reports support this view by providing evidence of poor internal control environments and the impact this has on the audit status of a departmental entity. So, while many reforms have been introduced, it is very clear that, at times, a slower pace of reform is required, if only to ensure that small gains are properly consolidated, thus readying the systems for further system changes. This rapid process of reform has not only left government officials behind, but civil society participation in the budget and budget process has also not necessarily kept pace with the reform agenda. Thus, although more and better information is available, CSOs are not making use of the glut of information to advocate for their policy and budgetary goals.

- Weak co-ordination among oversight institutions, constitutional bodies and the central government. The improvement of government financial management and systems is, to a large extent, dependent on how various oversight and constitutional bodies work together. It is not too hard to understand the reluctance to work together at the start of the new democracy, because most institutions had to establish themselves and the new government was grappling with a new policy agenda. A good example of this disconnect is the relationship between portfolio parliamentary committees at national and provincial levels. While functions such as education and health have concurrent competencies, there is very little evidence to suggest that issues of a policy nature (national) with implementation implications (provincial and local government) have filtered through in discussions at the provincial legislature level. While the National Council of Provinces (NCOP) deals with provincial issues at a national level, conditions that enhance policy and implementation continuity at the two levels of government have not materialised or resulted in tighter co-operation. Another example is the under-used nature of the PSC in the fight to ensure clean financial governance.

- Having a sub-national government with large expenditure commitments and virtually no revenue-raising powers. In the South African Constitution, spheres are referred to as interdependent. This is to emphasise the fact that the South African system can only work if there is a realisation that spheres are dependent on each other, and to convey the meaning that no sphere is subordinate to another. While the intergovernmental fiscal framework provides the revenues that are needed to make service delivery happen, provincial governments have little fiscal space to manoeuvre to take on provincial-specific concerns and issues. Also, given the pressure on the national government to realise campaign and policy promises, the future fiscal landscape could mean less and not more fiscal room for provinces. This has the unfortunate consequence of reducing provincial governments to administrations and removing the incentive to address unique provincial problems.

- Compliance mentality in implementing financial management reforms must be avoided. The issue of a compliance mentality or burden is not something that everyone subscribes to in the system. Many respondents (in both provincial and national departments) felt that this is indeed a reflection of the way government officials have approached the implementation of the PFMA, but the National Treasury has disputed this. However, if you accept the complaints made by many stakeholders, including the National Treasury, that many reports do not meet the required quality standards, one cannot help wondering whether this points to the existence of a compliance mentality. On paper, the penalties that the PFMA imposes are harsh and it is not inconceivable that most officials would want to avoid formal sanctions. What a compliance mentality does is separate the issue of good financial management practice from effective service delivery, which goes against the spirit and intent of the PFMA.

# Conclusion

In the Introduction to this paper, we raised the issue of how the implementation of a policy conditions its content and processes, and how, in some instances, implementation lessons may lead to a change in the policy's orientation. This view of the implementation process challenges the traditional view that neatly separates policy and implementation, and regards the latter as the practical arrangements needed to give effect to policy. Apart from the policy-implementation nexus, we also enquired whether the present consensus about the implementation of the PFMA (fiscal prudence achieved, great strides made in allocative efficiency and poor operational efficiency) still holds, or whether a re-description of that consensus view is in order.

On the first objective, the PFMA has remained substantively unchanged in spite of the implementation challenges faced over the last ten years. Our overall conclusion is that the law is well written and flexible enough to anticipate policy changes, but the key ingredients have been unchallenged and unchanged over the ten-year period of review. Recently, there have been calls for the amendment of the law, but the implementation evidence that we have presented does not support this view. Challenges related mostly to poor-quality finance staff, instability in staffing arrangements, and poor back-up systems (IT, M&E and non-financial reporting more generally), rather than provisions of the policy that are impossible to implement or were poorly conceived and, hence, impractical to implement. In other words, the people and systems that make full implementation of the PFMA possible have not been realised. What also enabled the framework legislation to remain relatively unscathed is the fact that the accompanying Treasury Regulations and circulars from the National Treasury tackled the practical aspects of the law head on. Our overall conclusion is that the implementation of the PFMA has had little impact on the integrity of the law itself. This view may change, but we are clearly not facing a situation where implementation evidence has forced a re-think of the overall intent and spirit of the PFMA.

In our examination of the consensus view on the implementation of the PFMA, we came to the following conclusions:

- Aggregate fiscal discipline has been achieved as a result of the introduction of the MTEF budget system and strong political backing and leadership. Our review has not suggested any evidence to the contrary.

- On the issue of allocative efficiency, the government has made great strides and our review concurs with most other reviews of this aspect. However, we argued that allocative efficiency gains at the sub-national level (provincial government) did not take place because of existing practices and efforts at that level. In fact, we argued that intergovernmental fora have largely brought about this situation, very much in the same vein as the old Function Committee. While this was good practice at the start of the new democracy, where aggressive re-prioritisation was needed, today requires a different approach to the issue of provincial discretion in the issues that these governments prioritise. Also, because of the small discretionary fiscal space at the provincial level, strategic planning skills are variable, thus further undermining the ability of provinces to address province-specific issues. If provinces are to remain a vital and vibrant level of government, the present intergovernmental fiscal architecture has to be re-thought.

- Operational efficiency gains have been unimpressive and, in this regard, we concur with other reviews. A poor disciplinary environment, variable AO performance, lack of measurement of the operational efficiency dimension, political interference in the in-year management of budgets, and insular departments that inconsistently follow up on SCOPA/AG recommendations have substantially weakened the operational efficiency of departments. We do, however, feel that the introduction of the FMCMM will have a positive impact on performance in this area as financial management benchmarks are now being developed. For the first time since the implementation of the PFMA, departments can now aim for targets laid out in improvement and action plans.

In our account of the implementation of the PFMA, we have established that earlier successes in the provision of timely and relevant information appear to have been facilitated by a capacity-building model based on the provision of uniform and clear financial information templates. In other words, the National Treasury played a substantial role in ensuring the information and transparency gains of the system. We question how far this model can be extended to accommodate higher-level goals (the so-called three e's) and, one of the issues to look at in terms of the future implementation of the PFMA is how the government intends to move departments to a higher rating on the financial capability scale.

South Africa has a long way to go to ensure that financial reforms are translated into service delivery gains. Progress in implementing reforms and making sure that citizens benefit is proving harder, yet the convergence of various government agencies in addressing financial governance is beginning to inspire the kind of confidence needed to overcome our financial governance challenges. On balance, despite the challenges, it appears that the PFMA has begun to make a difference and, if properly implemented, may still provide the ground for a fundamental transformation of public-sector service delivery.

# Endnotes

i    Major amendments and revisions to the Act included: repealing public audit provisions that were written into the PFMA after the enactment of the Public Audit Act, 2004 (No. 25 of 2004); amending Schedule 5 of the PFMA to include the remuneration and allowances of magistrates as a direct charge against the National Revenue Fund, in line with the remuneration of the President, Deputy President, Members of Parliament and Judges, after the enactment of the Judicial Officers Act, 2003 (No. 28 of 2003). With the listing of South African Airways, South African Express and the Broadband Infrastructure Company (Pty) Ltd as Major Public Entities, the enabling legislation of these entities amended Schedule 2 of the PFMA to include them as Major Entities. Data obtained in personal communication with the National Treasury in 2009.

ii    Schick (1998:2) defines aggregate fiscal discipline as 'Budget totals should be the result of explicit, enforced decisions; they should not merely accommodate spending demands. These totals should be set before individual spending decisions are made, and should be sustainable over the medium-term and beyond.' Allocative efficiency is defined as 'Expenditures should be based on government priorities and on effectiveness of public programs. The budget system should spur reallocation from lesser to higher priorities and from less to more effective programs.' Operational efficiency is defined as 'Agencies should produce goods and services at a cost that achieves ongoing efficiency gains and (to the extent appropriate) are competitive with market prices.'

iii    Function shifts have become an important strategy for the government as it tries to determine which sphere is best capable of delivering certain services. Grant payments, which used to be a provincial competency, are now being done by a national agency. Likewise, in education, adult basic education and training and further education and training, traditionally provincial functions, have been moved to the national level. In the same vein, it is not inconceivable that political pressures may push the national government to declare a larger portion of provincial and local spending as conditional spending, thus determining in an a priori manner where and on what additional resources should be spent. Such moves have obvious implications for allocative efficiency, and it is imperative that we understand the implications for service delivery and sub-national governments' ability to fulfil their constitutional mandates.

iv    These calculations were based on Provincial Budget Statements for the 2011/12 financial year.

v    Stories abound of corruption and the subversion of the normal processes of government in the South African commercial press. Despite the frequency of such high-profile political cases, one still needs an objective and accurate measure of the extent of political interference that leads to corruption and theft of scarce State resources.

vi    This point was demonstrated in a recent case in Gauteng where an independent school owner misused, abused and plainly stole a government subsidy that his school received. Although the owner had been roundly condemned and the Gauteng Department of Education was not seen as blameless, this incident is mainly a function of poor personnel provisioning, which makes it impossible to check the veracity and quality of quarterly financial reports sent by fund-receiving institutions. This also means that poor personnel provisioning plays into the hands of corrupt and criminally-minded officials and owners of private institutions that receive government funding. See http://www.iol.co.za/the-star/soweto/hawks-nab-pastor-red-handed-in-bribery-bid-1.1151609

vii    The PSC is mandated by sections 85(1)(a) and (e) of the PFMA and Treasury Regulation 4.3 to receive information from the AO on finalised disciplinary proceedings, which includes:

- the name and rank of the official against whom the proceedings were instituted;
- the charges, indicating the financial misconduct the official is alleged to have committed;
- the findings;
- any sanction imposed on the official; and
- any further action to be taken against the official, including criminal charges or civil proceedings (PSC, 2010:1).

viii   Ajam and Aron (2007) list fiscal stability, the creation of a transparent, constitutionally compliant intergovernmental fiscal relations system, improvements in the quality of fiscal data, and improved budget planning and control at all levels of government as visible signs of the overall budget-reform process. Folscher and Cole (2006) mention a more stable public-finance environment, improved political oversight and involvement, improved policy stability, and greater transparency as some of the immediate benefits of budget reforms, including the implementation of the PFMA.

ix     The OBI has been developed and is coordinated by the International Budget Partnership (IBP). It was first implemented in 2006 and, since then, there have been two further instalments of this growing budget transparency tool. It measures openness and transparency across the four stages of the budget process. It also measures the role of Parliament and the Supreme Audit institution, and is assessing the extent to which departmental entities comply with the results of audits. In essence, it probes whether the legislature and civil society as a whole has enough budget information to hold the Executive to account. In the 2010 version, South Africa was ranked first in the world, following its third and second positions in previous instalments of the OBI.

# References

Ajam, T. (2007) 'Integrating strategic planning and budgeting: A PFMA perspective' in *Auditing SA*, Summer 2007/8

Ajam, T. (2009) 'Budget oversight and poverty alleviation: opportunities and challenges' in Verwey, L., Lefko-Everett, K., Mohamed, A. & Zamisa, M. (2009) *Parliament, the budget and poverty in South Africa: A shift in power.* Cape Town: Idasa

Ajam, T. & Aron, J. (2007) 'Fiscal renaissance in a democratic South Africa' in *Journal of African Economies*, 16(5):745–781

Auditor General of South Africa (2009) 'General Report on the Audit Outcomes for the Departments, Constitutional Institutions, Public Entities and other Entities for the Financial Year 2007/08' http://www.agsa.co.za (accessed 10 November 2009)

Auditor-General of South Africa (2010) *Consolidated general report on the provincial audit outcomes*. Pretoria: Government Printers

Auditor-General of South Africa (2011) 'Report of the Auditor-General of South Africa to Parliament on a performance audit of the infrastructure delivery process at the provincial departments of Education and Health' http://www.agsa.co.za (accessed 01 November 2011)

Barberton, C. et al (2002) 'South Africa' in Folscher, A. (ed.) Budget Transparency and Participation: *Five African Case Studies. Cape Town:* Idasa

Brynard, P.A. (2005) 'Policy implementation: lessons for service delivery', a paper delivered at the 27th AAPAM annual roundtable conference, Livingstone, Zambia, 05–09 December 2005

Collaborative African Budget Reform Initiative (2004) 'Country Case Studies' 01-03 December 2004

Department of Cooperative Governance (2011), *Research Weekly Alert:* 05 August 2011

Department of Education (2002) 'Fifth Report to the President of South Africa on the State of Education' http://www.info.gov.za/view/DownloadFileAction?id=70239 (accessed 13 August 2011)

Department of Public Service and Administration (2010) *Delivery agreement for outcome 12: an efficient, effective and development oriented public service and an empowered, fair and inclusive citizenship*. Pretoria: Government Printers

European Commission (2008) 'Republic of South Africa Public Expenditure and Financial Accountability: Public Financial Management Performance Assessment Report' http://www.treasury.gov.za/publications/other/Final%20PEFA%20Report%20-%2029%20Sept%202008.pdf (accessed 30 September 2010)

Folscher, A. & Cole, N. (2006) 'South Africa: Transition to democracy offers opportunity for whole system reform' in *OECD Journal of Budgeting,* 6(2):1–37

Idasa (2009) 'Budget 2009: Still getting the balance right? PIMS Budget Paper 4' http://www.idasa.org (accessed 31 January 2010)

Kusi, N. (2006) 'Perspectives on financial management reforms in South Africa', Address delivered at the PFSA-AFReC Conference, East London, 2006

Maphiri, D (2011) 'Integrated in-year management system: a synthesis of seemingly unrelated issues' in *Southern African Journal of Accountability and Auditing Research*, 11:35–45

National Treasury (1999–2010) *Medium Term Budget Policy Statements*. Pretoria: Government Printers

National Treasury (2000) *Budget Review 2000*. Pretoria: Government Printers

National Treasury (2007) *Framework for Managing Programme Performance Information*. Pretoria: Government Printers

Nkoana, J. & Bokoda, P. (2009) 'Towards performance budgeting' in *South African Journal of Accountability and Auditing Research*, 9:49–55

Obadan, M.I. (2005) 'Challenges in the building of public service capacity in Africa', ACBF Working Paper, No. 5/March 2005

Public Service Commission (2010) *Overview on Financial Misconduct for the 2008/09 Financial Year*, Pretoria: Government Printers

Republic of South Africa (1999) *Public Finance Management Act, 1999* (No.1 of 1999). Pretoria: Government Printers

Schick, A. (1998) *A contemporary approach to public expenditure management*. Washington DC: World Bank Institute

Verwey, L. (2009) 'Pro-poor budgeting: general reflections and the South African situation' in Verwey, L., Lefko-Everett, K., Mohamed, A. & Zamisa, M. (2009) *Parliament, the budget and poverty in South Africa: A shift in power*. Cape Town: Idasa